BARNABY'S FRIENDS AND FANS HAVE SPOKEN...

"A SERIES OF COMIC STRIPS WHICH, LAID END TO END, REACH FROM HERE TO WHEREVER YOU WANT TO GO JUST ONCE BEFORE YOU DIE."
—*The New York Times*

"I WANT TO RECOMMEND *BARNABY* FOR THE CHRISTMAS STOCKINGS OF ALL PARENTS, UNCLES, AND OTHER ADULTS IN GOOD STANDING." —*Chicago Sunday Tribune*

"THE GREATEST BOOK SINCE *WAR AND PEACE*."
—*J.J. O'Malley*

"CROCKETT JOHNSON'S *BARNABY* COMES AS A BREATH OF SWEET, COOL AIR."
—*Life Magazine*

BARNABY BOOKS
Published by Ballantine Books

—AND LOTS MORE TO COME...

*Forthcoming

BARNABY #2

Mr. O'Malley and the Haunted House

by

CROCKETT JOHNSON

A Del Rey Book

Ballantine Books • New York

A Del Rey Book
Published by Ballantine Books

Copyright © 1985 by Random House, Inc.

Library of Congress Catalog Card Number: 85-90762

ISBN 0-345-32674-1

Designed by Gene Siegel

Manufactured in the United States of America

First Ballantine Books Edition: November 1985

A TIME THERE WAS
(and not so long ago)

when the world was very different for a five-year-old boy with an active mind.

There was no *Sesame Street* to immobilize him before a screen where puppets and clowns made games of letters and numbers. There were no Saturday cartoons to stultify his imagination with cliché supermen and wild events unrelated to his experience. Indeed, there was no television to hold him from the activities his mind and body needed to develop his growing abilities fully.

There were stories his parents might tell him or read to him, but those required mental creativity to flesh out the words.

It was a safer time, when a child might be free to explore the local haunted house with delighted shudders or wander into nearby woods to climb trees, chase squirrels, or pretend the shadows hid Indians, dragons, or ogres.

The brief radio broadcasts were filled with something about a war, of course; but without pictures of battle horrors, these were of little interest to a child. Anyhow, most adults preferred to listen to Stella Dallas, Vic and Sade, Edgar Bergen and Charlie McCarthy, Fred Allen, or Mr. Anthony who always knew the answers.

For the adults, this was a time when the Office of Civil Defense (OCD) was busy protecting us from the danger of bombs falling out of the skies (carried somehow by planes that could never have made the long round trip). There were blackouts with drills, sirens, and a large corps of volunteer air raid wardens. In this simpler world, the atom and hydrogen bombs did not yet exist.

But there were shortages, caused by the need for many things that had to be sent to our armed forces and allies across the seas. Ration boards doled out coupons for gasoline, tires, sugar, meat, and many other scarce items. Scrap metal drives were instituted, and people were encouraged to start victory gardens.

Of course, the shortages quickly produced a black market, with goods often supplied by the hijacking of trucks by the criminal element. Even stolen ration coupons were available— for a price.

It was a busy time for both adults and young children. It was a time when many things were done—some of them silly and some that were highly important.

Unfortunately, in the frantic events of those days, the simple faith of a boy named Barnaby and the importance of his Fairy Godfather, Jackeen J. O'Malley, were largely ignored.

They should not have been...

I got everybody's Christmas present all figured out, Mr. O'Malley, but I'm having a little trouble getting what I'm going to give Pop . . . You can make anything you want appear with your wand . . .

Yes, m'boy . . . Anything I ever want . . . Just a wave of my fine Havana magic wand.

Copyright 1942 Field Publications

Well, what I need for Pop is a—

Cushlamochree! Look at this! Are there some stamps in your father's writing desk, Barnaby!

Now where's that address again? . . . "Be a Ventriloquist . . . Frighten your friends . . . Slip this astounding device under your tongue and throw your voice . . . Send only ten cents in stamps for our Little Marvel Voice Thrower to"—Ah! Here it is—"Box 189506, Station D, Peoria" . . . That does it!

Now will you wave your magic wand and make Pop's present appear—

First I must send this communication off in the penny post, m'boy A voice thrower! What I've always wanted!

Hello, Barnaby. Has the postman left a package for your Fairy Godfather?

Gosh, Mr. O'Malley, you only wrote for that Little Marvel Voice Thrower yesterday.

12-19

But while you're here will you wave your wand and make a Christmas present for Pop appear? I decided to give him a dog ... It can lie by the fireplace at night when Pop smokes his pipe ... and days, I'll—

Certainly, m'boy. Just one dog?

Suppose we give him a team of sturdy huskies ... He can drive down to the office crying, "Mush!" ... Reminds me of my Yukon days and the time I was sitting with a friend named McGrew— poor fellow—in the Malemute Cocktail Lounge, and—But, say! I'm late! ...

I have an important appointment at the Elves, Leprechauns and Little Men's Chowder & Marching Society ... Send-off party for some of the boys who joined up with the Air Corps—as Gremlins ...

But what about Pop's Christmas present? ...

CROCKETT JOHNSON

Copyright 1942 Field Publications

3

Panel 1:
What a time I had helping Barnaby do his Christmas shopping! He refused to buy your present. He says "Mr. O'Malley," his mythical "Fairy Godfather" is going to produce something wonderful for you merely by waving his magic wand...

Fine. I'll depend on that.

Panel 2:
Then he insisted on buying a present for "Mr. O'Malley." He made such a fuss I had to let him buy that silly pixy a pair of 50-cent earmuffs!

Earmuffs? Let's see them.

Copyright 1943 Field Publications

Panel 3:
He's given them to "Mr. O'Malley" already... You see, his ears got cold flying around on his pink wings and there wasn't any point in waiting for Christmas and—

But what did Barnaby really do with them?

CROCKETT JOHNSON

Panel 4:
I'm depending on you for Pop's present, Mr. O'Malley, so wave your wand and—

Certainly, m'boy.... But now I want to rush down to the Elves, Gnomes, Leprechauns, and Little Men's Society and show off my elegant streamlined earmuffs...

4

Panel 1:

I'll make your father's Christmas present appear right now, Barnaby.... What was it you wanted to give him? Oh, yes—man's best friend—a horse.... I'll wave my wand.

No, Mr. O'Malley!

12-22 Copyright 1942 Field Publications

Panel 2:

I had a friend once named Man o' War. He was a horse.... Never lost a race.... Except.... Well.... You see, this day his jockey was taken ill at the post.... And I sprang into the saddle.... There was a steed in the race named Upset.... Gave him an unfair psychological advantage.

Not a horse! A dog!

Panel 3:

Yes, m'boy.... That's what he was, that Upset.... But he looked remarkably like a horse the day Man o' War and I—

I wan't to give Pop a DOG—not a horse...

CROCKETT JOHNSON

Panel 4:

Oh! Man's best friend—a dog! I knew a dog once.... Very celebrated canine... So famous Albert Payson Terhune did his biography.... Very interesting life story, Barnaby.... He was born in ...

But what about Pop's present...?

5

Hasn't the postman been here yet, Barnaby? . . . Why did I entrust the transportation of that Little Marvel Voice Thrower to the mails? . . . H I'd flown out to Box 189506, Station D, Peoria, myself, I would have—

Mr. O'Malley . . . Pop's present . . .

When that courier arrives, I shall demand to know what has stayed him in the swift completion of his appointed rounds . . . Obviously it can't be rain . . . nor snow . . . nor gloom of night . . . What else then? Fog? Flood? Slippery pavements?

Mr. O'Malley!

Barnaby, why do you harass your Fairy Godfather when he has so much on his mind? . . . Oh, very well! I'll get you that dog to give to your father for Christmas! I'll get that simple chore over with now!

Just wave your magic wand and the dog will appear—

CROCKETT JOHNSON Copyright 1943 Field Publications

RING!

RING!

Cushlamochree! The postman!

But the dog . . .

6

At last. It's arrived, m'boy! The Little Marvel Voice Thrower! . . . I have merely to slip it under my tongue and throw my voice anywhere I desire . . . Here! I'll throw it behind that tree! Listen!

12-24

Hello, Barnaby . . . I'm behind that tree over there! Amazing! Eh?

It didn't sound like it to me, Mr. O'Malley.

Mr. O'Malley, you promised to get that dog for Pop's Christmas present and I'm depending on it and tomorrow is—

Perhaps it takes a bit of practice . . . What did you say? Oh, yes . . . a dog . . .

I'm going off by myself for ten or fifteen minutes until I master the difficult art of ventriloquy . . . Stop worrying about that dog . . . Your Fairy Godfather promised him— Ergo—You as good as have him!

CROCKETT JOHNSON

Barnaby hardly looked at his presents!
... He still expects that imaginary Fairy
Godfather to turn up with a gift for you.

Maybe it's here already.
An imaginary present.

12-25

Hey, Mr. O'Malley! Gosh! You finally
got here! But where's Pop's present?

I can't stay a
minute, m'boy.

CROCKETT
JOHNSON

I've just learned that a friend of
mine who happens to be a werewolf
got picked up by the ASPCA again.

But it's Christmas!
And Pop hasn't got
a present from me—

Yes. Christmas. I can't allow my friend
to remain incarcerated on Christmas!
... I've always told him he can avoid
these recurring unpleasantnesses by
the simple expedient of purchasing
himself a license. But, no ... Anyway,
I must be off to effect his rescue ...

But ...

11

Of course that dog is wonderful and clever and goodnatured and all the things you say he is. Your Fairy Godfather wouldn't give you a dog without assuring himself of the beast's character and temperament . . . I trust he's in another part of the house?

12-31 Copyright 1942 Field Publications

Then I'll come in . . . I want to give you an astonishing demonstration of the science of ventriloquy, Barnaby, with the aid of my Little Marvel Voice Thrower . . . First, I'll throw my voice out the window! That Leprechaun, McSnoyd, suggested this trick.

If you cover your eyes, m'boy, the illusion is even more startling—

Ugh!

Okay . . . Go ahead Mr. O'Malley . . . Throw your voice out the window.

CROCKETT JOHNSON

CUSHLAMOCHREE!

Gosh! Marvelous, Mr. O'Malley!

13

Now that that dog has quieted down, I'd like to get in a little practice on my Little Marvel Voice Thrower ... Somehow word got around that I had written away for this amazing device and I was prevailed upon to give a ventriloquistic performance.

You're going to give a show?

Copyright 1943 Field Publications

Yes. Just for my colleagues at the Elves, Leprechauns, Gnomes and Little Men's Chowder & Marching Society. And I feel I need a bit more practice to achieve the degree of perfection they have grown to expect from any of my varied endeavors.

But it hasn't worked at all yet, has it, Mr. O'Malley?

Well, no, not YET ... But what I'm most worried about, Barnaby, is what sort of dummy to get for my act ... McSneyd, the Leprechaun, ventured the opinion that I didn't need a dummy, but inasmuch as ventriloquists always use them, I feel—

Say! I have it!

CROCKETT JOHNSON

I'll use Gorgon instead of a dummy! A sensational idea, m'boy! A TALKING DOG!

15

Imagine the cheers and bravos that will ring down the curtain on your old Fairy Godfather's ventriloquistic debut! A talking dog act! Amazing! . . . I'll have to begin giving some thought to movie and radio contracts . . . road companies . . .

That dumb beast is an excellent dummy. All he'll have to do is open his mouth a few times and I, with the aid of this Little Marvel Voice Thrower, will make him appear to speak. . . . I'll do it now . . .

Where's he going, Barnaby? Just when—

I think he's insulted because you said he was a good dummy.

CROCKETT JOHNSON Copyright 1943 Field Publications

Temperament!

Oh, the problems of an impressario . . .

17

But, Mr. O'Malley. Even if Gorgon can really talk, you still can use him in your show. Can't you, Mr. O'Malley?

Gee whiz... I can talk! Gee whiz...

1-9

How can he be the dummy in my utterly amazing ventriloquist act when he can talk? The discerning audience at the Elves, Leprechauns, Gnomes, and Little Men's Chowder & Marching Society will ask, "What's so amazing about this?"

Shouts of "Fraud!" will fill the hall... "O'Malley has rung in a real talking dog on us! Fake!" they will scream... No, m'boy. I daren't go through with it.

Gosh!

Copyright 1942 Field Publications

But the show must go on. ...Luckily I have my card tricks to fall back upon...

Gosh!

CROCKETT JOHNSON

21

23

25

And then there's the one about the man who ordered a special cake and he was so fussy about the shape of it that he had it done over four times and when the baker said, "Now that it is finally okay, where shall I deliver this cake?"

... The man said, "Oh, I'll eat it here."

Yes. We've heard that one, too! Barnaby, isn't there same way we can make this shaggy dog stop his shaggy dog stories? I came here to tell you of ...

CROCKETT JOHNSON

This one should be told in dialect ... But, anyway ...

This will stop him, Mr. O'Malley. Watch. PLAY DEAD, Gorgon!

Okay. Well, this Cockney fellow came home one night and found a giraffe in his bathroom. "Bli'me," he said —

I came here to tell you — Say! This talking dog IS amazing ... He out-talks your Fairy Godfather!

Panel 1:
It seems this fellow came to the factory and ordered an egg-shaped pool table, six feet high, and covered with bear skin...

If you don't stop telling shaggy dog stories, I'll put you in the cellar...

Copyright 1943 Field Publications

Panel 2:
They said they could make it for him in three months, and the man paid half what it was going to cost and went away, but in a couple of weeks he was drafted...

What I was going to say, Barnaby, was...

Panel 3:
So if you want an egg-shaped pool table, six feet high, and covered with bear skin, you can get it cheap...

Now what were you saying, Mr. O'Malley?

Panel 4:
Last night I happened to fly past that deserted house up the road and I saw a light in the window and it reminded me of that old shaggy dog story of the Irishman and the Banshee—Stop me if—

A light in that old haunted house?

CROCKETT JOHNSON

Mom . . . Is it all right for me to kind of look around in that haunted house up the road?

The Jackson place? It's not haunted, Barnaby. People say that about all old deserted buildings.

But you stay away from it . . . It's too far, for one thing, and if you prowl around in a ramshackle building by yourself, you'll fall and get hurt . . .

I wouldn't go by myself, Mom.

That's right . . . If you're curious about it you can investigate it when some older, responsible person is with you.

Sure . . . I wouldn't go except with a very responsible person . . .

Okay, Mr. O'Malley. Mom says I can go with you.

CROCKETT JOHNSON   Copyright 1943 Field Publications

The grounds are in a terrible state of disrepair... And you've been up to this old house all by yourself, little girl? Dangerous... Very dangerous... Why the place must be rife with pitfalls...

There's only that open cistern over there.

Precisely the sort of thing I mean... Be very careful now... Just follow O'Malley.

You realize how lucky you are, Barnaby, when you see the perils that continually confront other children who haven't got Fairy Godfathers watching over them...

Hey! Look out, Mr. O'Malley!

Cushlamochree!

Are you all right, Mr. O'Malley? Can you climb out of there?

I'm all right but these Walls weren't meant for climbing... Don't worry, I'll think of something...

1-25

My Fairy Godfather won't have any trouble getting out of that cistern, Jane... He'll probably do it by magic. ...He'll just wave his wand...or— Why, of course! He can FLY out!

Cúshlamochree!

I can't fly up... There's no room for a take-off... But I'll think of a way.

He'll think of something quite remarkable, Jane... He's very resourceful.

CROCKETT JOHNSON Copyright 1943 Field Publications

I've got it, m'boy! You kids run home and get a ROPE!

34

I don't see anything so very remarkable about your Fairy Godfather being able to get out of a well with a clothesline, Barnaby. Anybody could do that... And I ought to go home... It's getting dark.

But you want to see Mr. O'Malley do the rope trick, don't you? He'll throw one end up in the air and he'll climb right up... It's VERY remarkable...

Jane is awfully anxious to see you do the rope trick, Mr. O'Malley... Shall I throw the rope down now?

Don't even need the whole rope, m'boy... Just one end of it.

Now pull hard on the other end... Up we go!

39

Gosh, Mr. O'Malley. If your friend Gus here didn't make those lights appear in that old house, who did?

Oh, dear.

It's still a mystery. We must continue my investigation.

Now? I'd better go home, Mr. O'Malley. Mom and Pop will think something very unusual has happened to me . . .

No. Not now. Tomorrow's another day . . . But what about poor Gus, m'boy?

He's afraid to go back to that haunted house . . . So it's up to your Fairy Godfather to find him other lodgings . . . Shouldn't be difficult with my influence and wide circle of — Say! I have it! Just the place!

Where, Mr. O'Malley?

Oh, I'm being such a bother!

YOUR HOUSE, Barnaby!

Well, okay, but, gosh . . .

CROCKETT JOHNSON

What's that, Mrs. Shultz? Your little girl has just come in? But Barnaby's not with her? Where has she been until this hour? And ask her if Barnaby was—

It's no use. Mrs. Shultz says Jane is too excited to talk sense. She told some nonsensical story about a ghost eating up Barnaby's Fairy Godfather... Mr. Shultz is coming over and we'll start a search—

SLAM

CROCKETT JOHNSON

Don't be alarmed, Pop. The ghost didn't eat up Mr. O'Malley... Jane was imagining things.

BARNABY!

What happened—

*Copyright 1943 Field Publications

The ghost turned out to be quite a nice fellow... an old friend of Mr. O'Malley's named Gus... Gus was scared out of the haunted house by strange noises and—

Jane was imagining things... This is how it REALLY happened.

Oh, Mr. Shultz. We telephoned you but you'd already left. Barnaby finally got home! So you and John won't have to search for him.

Sit down awhile, anyhow.

I've got a search of my own on my hands, Baxter... Eleven truckloads of coffee have been hijacked on the highway in the past month... Drivers held up, ordered out onto the road and the trucks stolen... They're always found, abandoned and empty... My insurance company and the police are convinced the gang is operating right from a base in this neighborhood...

Copyright 1945 Field Publications

If it's in this neighborhood, someone should have noticed any strange goings on in a nearby house... But that's the trouble with people nowadays. A lot of them wouldn't notice strange goings on if it happened in their own homes under their own noses.

Yes, m'boy, there are strange goings on in that old deserted house... Your Fairy Godfather will have a look around there when I pick up your guest's luggage in the morning... By the way I made Gus the Ghost comfortable in your cellar on a nice big basket of clean laundry.

CROCKETT JOHNSON

Shouldn't we tell the cops about that Coffee Fiend in the old haunted house, Mr. O'Malley?

Yes! Police protection! I'll be glad to make a formal complaint and—

COFFEE

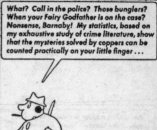

What? Call in the police? Those bunglers? When your Fairy Godfather is on the case? Nonsense, Barnaby! My statistics, based on my exhaustive study of crime literature, show that the mysteries solved by coppers can be counted practically on your little finger ...

2-8

If we are to find out what the Fiend is up to we can't have any clumsy policemen unwittingly informing him of our intent. ...No, m'boy. A problem like this calls for the brilliant analytical brain of an Auguste Dupin, an Hercule Poirot, a Doctor Thorndyke, a Nero Wolfe, or a Philo Vance ... Lucky I'm here, aren't we?

CROCKETT JOHNSON

While we're in the kitchen, Barnaby, I think a bit of bodily nourishment might aid my analytical thinking on that haunted house mystery... What luck! Tuna fish! Brain food!

2-10

As Sherlock Holmes once remarked to your Fairy Godfather, "Alimentary, my dear Watson"... Get it, m'boy? A clever pun... Holmes said, "ALImentary, my—

But why did he call you "Watson," Mr. O'Malley?

He thought it was my name, of course... He deduced it... It was dark in the larder of his Baker Street flat. You see my good friend Professor Moriarity, who always ate there, forgot his lantern that night and only the light of my fine Havana wand—

Your magic wand!

CROCKETT JOHNSON

Mr. O'Malley! I know how you can find out what the Fiend is doing in the haunted house!

Copyright 1943 Field Publications   CROCKETT JOHNSON

Panel 1:
Yes, of course, my Fairy Godfather's Handy Pocket Guide tells how to vanquish Fiends... I'll look in the index... "Vanquishing of: Demons; Evil Spirits"—It's an alphabetical listing... Here!—"Fiends, page 28."

Panel 2:
Then you can go right into the haunted house and find out what the Fiend is doing there! Just wave your magic wand at him and make him CONFESS!

Not a very sporting way to solve a mystery, m'boy.

Panel 3:
Ellery Queen wouldn't approve of it... Makes no use at all of my brilliant analytical brain.

But, gosh! Other detectives haven't got magic wands!

Panel 4:
I'll get Gorgon and wake up Gus and we'll go with you! We'll get Jane, too. She won't want to miss seeing THIS!

49

... And George's insurance company and the police think it's very probable that these gangsters who have been holding up the coffee trucks have headquarters right in this vicinity ... And that these tons of stolen coffee may be stored in a house right in this very neighborhood ...

Yes ... Mr. Shultz told John about it the other night ...

Speaking of coffee, Mrs. Shultz, won't you stay for a cup of tea?

Let me help ... Where's the sugar? Here in the pantry? ... Yes, I guess everyone is out of coffee most of the time now ... Except a few hoarders ... But hoarders are caught every—

CROCKETT JOHNSON Copyright 1943 Field Publications

EEEEEEEK!

COFFEE

51

So we called Mr. Shultz... He says the twenty-pound bag of coffee we found in our pantry is evidently part of the stolen supply his insurance company and the police have been looking for!

...And the only possible explanation is that Barnaby found it in that old deserted house and brought it home... Probably to surprise us... but I can't find him. He's disappeared again! And Mrs. Shultz can't find Jane either!

...Mr. Shultz has called the police and they're coming to search the deserted house... And if it IS the gangsters' headquarters and if these two kids have gone there again... Oh, John! ...Something terrible might happen!

If Barnaby's there something terrible will happen all right! ...Probably to the gangsters!

But I'll be right home, Ellen.

CROCKETT JOHNSON

Like I am saying to myself just last night ... "Egboit," I say, "This ain't no position for a active guy like I am. Sitting around in an old haunted house watching a lot of hot java. Egboit, you might get to become whacky and commence talking to myself even." When I hear this, I say, "Egboit, you are very right about this matter. You are talking to myself at this very instant!" So, you see, Boss, it's—

COFFEE

I'm moving the coffee tomorrow, Eggy. Stick it out one more day ... You're all right ... A touch of nerves, that's all.

Probably them "coffee nerves" they talk about ... But I ain't whacky, huh, Boss?

Quit worrying about it ... You're not whacky until you begin seeing things.

CROCKETT JOHNSON Copyright 1943 Field Publications

Hurry up, Gus. Everybody else is inside the house already.

It's a very good thing Mr. O'Malley, my Fairy Godfather, could give such a fine description of a Fiend ... Green, with a long tail with a hook on it and red shining eyes ... Otherwise I wouldn't know what to look for in this house.

2-17

Gosh! Look at all that coffee!

But I don't see the Fiend ... I'll look in this room next.

Somethin's outside in the hall ... Listen, Boss!

Copyright 1943 Field Publications

CROCKETT JOHNSON

Gosh! ... I didn't know anybody lived here. I'm looking for a—

It's a little kid!

56

57

I suppose you've seen the newspapers, Barnaby... The usual thing. The police have taken all credit for recovering the stolen coffee and capturing those gangsters... Haha. Amusing, isn't it?

Didn't they even mention you?

No. Not a line... But that's the way we great detectives work, m'boy... We solve a baffling case and quietly step out of the limelight, renouncing the plaudits of the press... No one learns the true facts until he comes upon our book in his drug store lending library...

A book?

It would make a fine thriller, wouldn't it? "The Case of the Hot Coffee Ring?"... A pity your Fairy Godfather is too busy to do it... But it really should be written... Say! I don't suppose you know a good Ghostwriter?

Gosh. I don't know any Ghosts, Mr. O'Malley... Only your friend Gus.

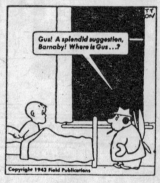

Gus! A splendid suggestion, Barnaby! Where is Gus...?

Barnaby, I like your house much better than that unheated old mansion. I'll do my haunting here from now on—

Huh?

Gus. I want you to help me with a little book I'm getting together.

You're moving in for good? But we haven't got much room and, gosh, Mom won't—

I'm sorry, O'Malley, but I won't have anything to do with that type of venture.

Not that kind of book, Gus...

I know it's a small house, Barnaby. But it's nice and cozy... And I'll do a very fine haunting job here... Oh, nothing ostentatious, of course. Just a simple routine... Well-modulated moans and very few shrieks... All in good taste...

But...

It's literature...

Mr. O'Malley. Can't you explain to Gus—

Yes. I'll explain to him all about the book he and I are to collaborate on. We'll get right to work... Great, him living here, isn't it, m'boy?

But, Mr. O'Malley...Mom won't like having Gus live with us...For one thing he hasn't got any ration allowance and besides—

Quiet, Barnaby...Please...This book, Gus, will be the thrilling account of my exposé of the hijackers...I'm calling it The Amazing Case of the Hot Coffee Ring...by Jackeen J. O'Malley, The Scourge of the Underworld. ...We'll want to get started writing it immediately.

But, O'Malley...If I'm not welcome here...

Barnaby...Surely you don't want to block your old Fairy Godfather's path to literary fame and fortune and free luncheons at the Dutch Treat Club! Of course you don't...

But...

All I'm asking is board and lodging for my Ghostwriter, the loan of your Dad's portable typewriter, and a few reams of paper...And for that I shall present you with a copy of my titanic work as soon as it's off the press—a first edition—clean dust jacket—and autographed!

Will it have pictures in it?

CROCKETT JOHNSON

It's difficult, recalling the events of one's early life ... I should have taken notes as I went along ... You've got how I was born in a log cabin, Gus? ... And how I got out of my cradle one night to play a cadenza for my most recent concerto on the grand piano in our music room? ... And the time I was showing a kid on our block by the name of Paul Bunyan a few tricks with my hatchet and I chopped down that cherry tree? ... And then how I toddled up to the pater and said, "Oh, Father, dear Father, come home with me now ..."

Bzzz zzzz zzz zz zzzz zzz ...

Copyright 1943 Field Publications

We'll want at least a passing reference to the time I held my finger in the dike ... While I stood on the burning deck ...

Barnaby. Please be quiet ... I realize how exciting it is for you to hear me relating my amazing life story, but—

Bzzzzz zz zzz zzzzz ... Okay.

CROCKETT JOHNSON

Cushlamochree! Where are you kids going?

We're going up and watch the ickles dropping off the porch roof, Mr. O'Malley.

3-8

No. My book isn't completed, Barnaby. Gus finished the first chapter and he's resting a while on your bed ... Oh, say—

How's this pose, m'boy? ... For the frontispiece of my autobiography. ... Possibly a bit too austere, eh?

Or should the camera emphasize the poet and scholar in me? ... Perhaps if I wore a pair of—Gus, let me have your glasses a moment.... Ah, how's this?

Careful of those bifocals, O'Malley.

Copyright 1943 Field Publications

Or an informal flash, catching me as I stress a profound philosophical point with a wave of my spectacles.

I can't read and write without them...

You look just like a mayor—

CROCKETT JOHNSON

3-10

O'Malley. If anything happens to them...

What's that, Gus?—Oops!

... I can't finish your life story!

Cushlamochree!

Gesh! Has Gus got his glasses fixed, Mr. O'Malley?

No. He's merely wearing the frames . . . A precaution against any possible invitations to fisticuffs at the Elves, Leprechauns, Gnomes and Little Men's Chowder & Marching Society . . . But he'll have new lenses soon.

I hope so, O'Malley.

3-12   Copyright 1943 Field Publications

I've borrowed your father's briefcase to transport my unfinished life story. I want to show the manuscript around at the club to arouse interest in the dinner at which I shall read several exciting and inspirational excerpts . . . There'll be a rush for tickets and the tidy profit from the affair will more than pay for repairing Gus's glasses . . . So he can continue writing my book.

What affair, Mr. O'Malley?

Biggest event of the social season, m'boy!

. . . The First Annual Jackeen J. O'Malley Testimonial Dinner!

CROCKETT JOHNSON

Panel 1: I'll take this last poster out and put it up right away. I don't like being near that Chowder & Marching Club after dark... Oh, by the way, O'Malley...A couple of Gnomes asked about the "Entertainment"...What's it going to be?

FIRST ANNUAL
JACKEEN J. O'MALLEY
TESTIMONIAL DINNER
ENTERTAINMENT
ALL TOP ACTS

3-13

Panel 2: Well, there's a reading from my work in progress... I'll do that myself, of course... Songs by a silver-throated tenor... Dancing by a fine soft-shoe artist...: Boogie Woogie piano playing ...All top acts, Gus... And, oh, yes! I almost forgot... A most astounding demonstration of prestidigitation!

Copyright 1943 Field Publications

CROCKETT JOHNSON

Panel 3: Prestidigitation? Dear me. You're not going to attempt to do that card trick again....Not before all those people!

Nonsense. I do it perfectly! I'll admit my dance routine may need a bit of polishing.

Panel 4: My left hand is a bit weak on several of my Boogie Woogie numbers... And I'll have to run over my vocal selections...

Gosh! My Fairy Godfather is the whole show!

75

I intend to help out by singing at your testimonial dinner, O'Malley... You know I was once with the Metropolitan Opera—

Gosh! If Gus was in opera—

3-16

He didn't SING, m'boy... He was there that year of the big deficit when the Met tried to cater to more popular tastes by installing a Phantom... No thanks, Gus... I had better take care of the singing... I'll do everything...

Very well! Then you won't need me to clean the hall and take tickets either! And wait on the tables! Very well! So I'll say "Goodbye," O'Malley. Goodbye!

GUS!

He's mad!

CROCKETT JOHNSON

Copyright 1943 Field Publications

CROCKETT JOHNSON

3-18

3-19

CROCKETT
JOHNSON

I'm taking these lozenges for my throat, m'boy ... Can't afford to have anything go wrong with my voice before the dinner ... Great strain ... Rehearsing speeches and singing with that quartet ... Have one?

Gosh, thanks, Mr. O'Malley.

Very tasty, aren't they? ... Another thing: I just realized that the Vernal Equinox is here ... Time to remove my earmuffs. ... I'm packing them away here in your dresser ... Brought a bag of mothballs—

UGH!

3-20

CROCKETT JOHNSON

Mr. O'Malley! You've been eating the MOTHBALLS!

Naturally, McSnoyd, I didn't sing as loud as I can ... I'm giving you and the other members of this quartet a chance ... I have a hereditary advantage over you. My mother was a Banshee ... A powerful coloratura who could reach High C and—

Don't waste no wind on them alibis, pal.

Copyright 1943 Field Publications

Show that invisible old Leprechaun how loud you CAN sing, Mr. O'Malley.

Very well, m'boy ... But be careful of flying decibles ... I'll breathe deep—

Don't make us all deaf, O'Malley ...

3-23

CROCKETT JOHNSON

I don't hear ANYTHING, Mr. O'Malley!

He done it! ... I AM deaf!

83

Mr. O'Malley! Did you lose your voice?

It ain't lost, kid. It just finally wore out.

Oh, dear!

Probably them is harsh woids, O'Malley, but—

3·24

CROCKETT JOHNSON

Don't argue with that invisible old Leprechaun, Mr. O'Malley ... Pop has some throat medicine and ...

Oh, so you won't talk, O'Malley ...

Copyright 1943 Field Publications

85

Yes, Barnaby. Dogs hear some noises people can't hear. . . . Their range of hearing is slightly different than ours. . . . The threshold of sound is—

I see, Pop.

3-29

That's what the child needs to curb that imagination of his. . . . Simple clear, realistic explanations of the things he observes that puzzle him.

Yes. . . .

Scientific facts will break down his belief in that little man with wings and talking animals and all this imaginary nonsense. . . .

I guess so. . . .

CROCKETT JOHNSON

Gorgon CAN hear you, even if I can't, Mr. O'Malley. . . . Pop says it's a scientific fact. . . .

Sure.

Here's Gus and that invisible old Leprechaun.

FIRST ANNUAL
JACKEEN J.
O'MALLEY
TESTIMONIAL
DINNER
CANCELLED

3-31

O'Malley! I hear you've cancelled the testimonial dinner! Oh, dear! It would have been a TERRIFIC success! EVERYBODY was going!

They said they wouldn't miss it for the woild!

They were going? Even though Mr. O'Malley's lost his voice and they couldn't hear his speeches?

Çoitainly...

Copyright 1943 Field Publications

That's what they meant they wouldn't miss for the woild, kid. . . . Not hearing O'Malley!

CROCKETT JOHNSON

So the clambake's off, eh, O'Malley? . . . On account of you losing your verce? . . . I'll be slogging along then. Back to the old gold pile.

And I think I'll run along, too, O'Malley.

Are you going to help the invisible Leprechaun to guard his treasure, Gus?

No. . . . I'm going down to the war plant. . . . There's a situation open . . . On the graveyard shift, and—

Aw revoy, O'Malley . . . as the Free Frenchman says. . . . Don't take no wooden horses. . . .

CROCKETT JOHNSON

FIRST ANNUAL
JACKEEN J.
O'MALLEY
TESTIMONIAL
DINNER
CANCELLED

Pop, Mr. O'Malley, my Fairy Godfather, was going to do that with some magic words, but his voice gave out—

We'll do it the hard way, son.

I think that's a big enough Victory Garden for a boy to handle. Smooth out the soil with a rake, Barnaby...And then decide what you want to plant...I'll be right back.

Okay, Pop.

Mr. O'Malley will feel bad about us doing the hardest part without him...Now I only have to pick what to plant...Corn or beans or—

Mangos, m'boy! Plant some nice tasty mangos!

Copyright 1943 Field Publications

CROCKETT JOHNSON

Panel 1:

Mangos are a "must" in any Victory Garden, Barnaby... Can't make chutney without them, you know... And even the best curries, without—

I was going to plant beans...

Panel 2:

Beans! How unimaginative!

In a story, a beanstalk get so big a boy named Jack climbed up it and met a Giant and got a bag of gold.

Panel 3:

A tall tale, m'boy... One of a large category of wish-fulfillment yarns invented by hopelessly impoverished peasantries... We must be realistic about this garden.... Down to earth! ...I'll be back... with mango seeds.

4-6

Panel 4:

CROCKETT JOHNSON

I was going to grow beans, Pop. But I guess I'll be sensible and plant mangos.

Huh?

You can't raise mangos, Barnaby. Mangos grow on trees... And only in tropical countries... Where did you ever get an idea like that?

But Mr. O'Malley, my Fairy Godfather—

4-7

I thought so! Look, son. Whose advice are you going to follow? Mine? Or that of an imaginary creature out of your dreams?

But—Okay, Pop. I'll plant beans.

Copyright 1942 Field Publications

Not a single mango seed at the hardware shop, Barnaby... Such a demand for them, I suppose— Say! What is it you're planting?

Beans...

Beans! Barnaby! Whose advice are you following in this matter?

But... Gosh, Mr. O'Malley.

CROCKETT JOHNSON

96

Very well, Barnaby... Far be it from your Fairy Godfather to cause enmity between father and son... Plant beans in your Victory Garden if he wants to be stubborn about the matter.

But those seeds he's given you look like a decidedly inferior variety. If you must grow beans I might—But no—I must not interfere... Go on. Plant them.

Have you got better ones, Mr. O'Malley?

It happens I have a packet of very superlative type quality beans which were presented to me by an ex-congressman friend. ...From his own private beanbag. And I might part with—But, no...

CROCKETT JOHNSON

Very well, m'boy. I'll get them for you.... After all, we want this garden to be something exceedingly unusual, don't we?

Well...

Panel 1:
Haw! Gee! Straight furrows, Gorgon!

This isn't the way Pop said to plant seeds, Mr. O'Malley.

. . . This shouldn't happen to a cat.

4-9

Panel 2:
We O'Malleys have always had a knack for horticulture, Barnaby . . . Luther Burbank wouldn't pick up a pair of pruning shears without my advice . . . And Doctor Carver—

Gosh! That's Pop's mineral water . . .

Copyright 1943 Field Publications.

Panel 3:
Yes . . . The little seedlings need minerals . . . Even Third Cousin Malachy O'Malley, the family blacksheep, has ability . . . He's quite an expert in his field . . .

Does he grow things?

Panel 4:
No. As I said, he's a blacksheep. Third Cousin Malachy withers rosebushes. . . Well, m'boy, that's about all there is to making a garden . . . Now we'll just stand around here and watch it grow!

CROCKETT JOHNSON

99

101

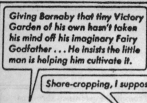

Giving Barnaby that tiny Victory Garden of his own hasn't taken his mind off his imaginary Fairy Godfather . . . He insists the little man is helping him cultivate it.

Share-cropping, I suppose.

Pop! Mr. O'Malley, my Fairy Godfather thinks we ought to put a scarecrow up in my garden and he's going to borrow one of your suits . . .

Don't be funny about this, John.

Why not have this Mr. O'Malley of yours stand out there himself, son? Won't he make a good scarecrow?

Me? A scarecrow? Cushlamochree!

Come back, Mr. O'Malley! Pop only—

HE'S GONE! . . . POP! YOU INSULTED MR. O'MALLEY!

Now you've done it . . .

CROCKETT JOHNSON

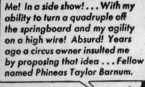

Me! In a side show! ... With my ability to turn a quadruple off the springboard and my agility on a high wire! Absurd! Years ago a circus owner insulted me by proposing that idea ... Fellow named Phineas Taylor Barnum.

4-21

Maybe the circus man thought people would pay lots of money just to look at you ... Even if you didn't turn somersaults ...

Well, he did have a reputation for never missing a trick, this Barnum ... But aside from the humiliation of being ogled in a side show, I couldn't condone preying on people's gullibility.

CROCKETT JOHNSON

He intended to conceal my wings in some manner and pass me off as a MIDGET!

Gosh!

108

110

111

Open wider, Gorgon ...

Ugh!

Try putting HIS head in YOUR mouth, Mr. O'Malley.

It's no use, Barnaby ... I can't practice my lion-taming act without lions ... We'll have to hunt one up in the forest ...

In our woods? There aren't any lions in it.

Copyright 1943 Field Publications

Don't contradict your Fairy Godfather, m'boy. I've seen their green eyes at night in the underbrush ... Only my agility has saved me from being pounced upon often.

We'll set off on our safari late at night ... Real sport, moonlight lion-hunting ...

I'd better ask Mom first ...

CROCKETT JOHNSON

114

115

In that underbrush! Listen! It's a LION!

Stand back, m'boy! . . . Out of the path of its charge!

It's another rabbit . . .

Maybe there aren't any lions around here . . .

Nonsense . . . Lions are nocturnal animals . . . They roam around in the night . . . And it's night now, isn't it?

CROCKETT JOHNSON

GRRROARRR

You're right, Mr. O'Malley! It's a LION!

117

Everybody's working putting up the tent.

COMBINED CIRCUS

They've left these lion wagons unattended! . . . How careless! And the cages are not even properly secured! Look, m'boy. If these handnuts happened to become unscrewed . . . This chain could work loose . . . See?

5·3

Copyright 1943 Field Publications

Then what prevents the bolt from sliding back? . . . Like this . . . And THEN if anyone jostled against the gate . . .

Hey Mr. O'Malley!

CROCKETT JOHNSON

Look!

Elephants!

Well, we did find some lions, Mr. O'Malley. But they were circus lions and in closed cages . . .

Yes. Our big game hunt was rather disappointing. Too bad . . . But that's the luck of the chase, m'boy.

5·4

Not that I have experienced this sort of thing often, Barnaby. As a matter of fact, I don't believe Bring-'Em-Back-Alive O'Malley ever before has returned from a lion hunt in this predicament.

CROCKETT JOHNSON

The lion followed Mr. O'Malley, my Fairy Godfather, and me home from the woods! I didn't dream it! I promised to take care of him for Mr. O'Malley.

5-12

Gosh!

We won't argue about it any more . . . Look! They're coaxing the lion into the cage with that big leg of meat . . . And that's only his BREAKFAST!

About how many red stamps is that, Mom?

CROCKETT JOHNSON

Okay. I guess I'll let the circus take care of him. .

Couldn't convince my cynical colleagues at the Little Men's Chowder & Marching Society about my lion-taming. They wouldn't believe I have a lion! ... Wouldn't even come to see!

Mr. O'Malley ...

5-13

I promised them that, within the hour, they will find me in the club lobby with my head in a lion's mouth! ... And, to teach the scoffers a lesson, I accepted wagers on it ...

But ...

CROCKETT JOHNSON

Your Fairy Godfather and his lion will rouse that allegedly social organization out of its smug skepticism, Barnaby ...

But ... Listen!

Copyright 1943 Field Publications

The circus men came and took him, Mr. O'Malley. You haven't got a lion anymore.

Cushlamochree!

But when the circus men got the lion out of the cellar, they gave us six free tickets, Mr. O'Malley

Six Oakleys? Well, well . . .

5-14

An attempt to modify my wrath . . . Well, I will no longer consider an affiliation with the show . . . But I might attend a performance . . . Whom shall we take on the four other tickets? . . . Gus McSnoyd—

But . . .

But the man gave them to Pop, Mr. O'Malley . . . And he and Mom are going with me. . . . And they've invited Mr. and Mrs. Shultz and Jane—

Three. Four. Five . . . SIX!

Copyright 1943 Field Publications

CROCKETT JOHNSON

But Mr. O'Malley . . .

131

132

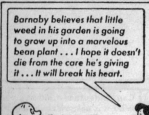

Barnaby believes that little weed in his garden is going to grow up into a marvelous bean plant . . . I hope it doesn't die from the care he's giving it . . . It will break his heart.

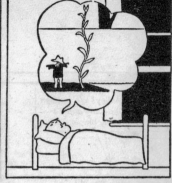

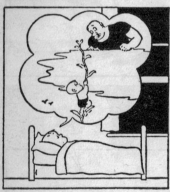

Barnaby! Prepare yourself for terrible news! Torn up by the roots! The beanstalk!

CROCKETT JOHNSON

135

A Giant chewed it up last night, Pop. It's a magic beanstalk—

A rabbit did this, son . . .

. . . And if I'd argued with Barnaby, he'd have quoted "Mr. O'Malley" as his authority and agreed with him.

Hey, Pop.

Of course he always agrees with "Mr. O'Malley" . . . He invented that Fairy Godfather, so naturally —

CROCKETT JOHNSON

We're going to find that Giant and ask him if he did it . . . Mr. O'Malley and I were arguing . . . He says it was a rabbit, too . . .

No, Barnaby. We haven't completed our plan for the post-war world yet. . . . Atlas became rather difficult to work with . . .

You know how highstrung Mental Giants are . . . And when his slide rule broke, while I was attempting to do Long Division with it—

CROCKETT JOHNSON

But luckily I thought of another approach to the problem of dividing up a world. Your father won't mind if I borrow this . . . ?

Pop plans battles on it, Mr. O'Malley.

But I promised Atlas . . . He's waiting outside . . . And now, a saw from the toolchest . . .

Gosh . . . No!

Copyright 1943 Field Publications

143

The globe broke on his head!

Cushlamochree! I must soothe Atlas's feelings.

FEE! FI! FO! FUM!

6·3   Copyright 1943 Field Publications

Barnaby! What have you done!

My Fairy Godfather, Mr. O'Malley, and a Giant—a MENTAL one—they were—

Stop cross-examining the poor child, John! He walked in his sleep and he bumped the table—

Impossible . . .

Hush, John . . . It's all right now Barnaby. You were dreaming—

But—

But—

CROCKETT JOHNSON

We'll find your father in a jiffy if he's living with people named Baskerville.

He went there after he got ruled off all the dogtracks.

6-12

Copyright 1943 Field Publications

Only one Baskerville in the book—Mrs. Jenny H.—9-4-6-1.

His name's "Rover" . . .

Yes, but they probably have no reason to list your father in the directory and—Hello? Mrs. Baskerville? . . . Have you a dog? What's his name? . . . Oh, I see—Well, thank you very much . . . Yes, you might call this a "survey" . . .

CROCKETT JOHNSON

They have a dog?

Yes, but it can't be Gorgon's father . . . Her name's "Toots."

No. That's not him.

Panel 1:
Even if your father can't read, Gorgon, he'll have a friend—an educated man or woman—who will see the advertisement and—

Maybe he hasn't got any friends.

6-15

Panel 2:
Nonsense. . . . A dog is man's best friend and it takes two to make a friendship. . . . I'll start preparing copy, m'boy, and when your mother gets home she can insert the ad.

Panel 3:
And we must give thought to our choice of media, as I always told the tycoons who sought my advice on their enormous national campaigns when I ran the high-powered B. B. D. & O'Malley agency. . .

CROCKETT JOHNSON

Panel 4:
I invariably urged expending their entire budgets on space in the personal columns of the *Saturday Review of Literature*—

I heard Mom come in, Mr. O'Malley. . .

Copyright 1943 Field Publications

John! The most awful thing! I lost my bag somewhere downtown. Mrs. Shultz and I called every place we've been but it hasn't turned up. And my watch was in it, too.

I'll tell Mom Mr. O'Malley's idea about advertising for your father, Gorgon. We'll find him for you all right.

Don't go to a lot of trouble.

CROCKETT JOHNSON

"... small reward. Finder please phone Main 0672." Yes. Just one insertion....

Huh?

6·16

Mr. O'Malley! ... Mom put the ad in already!

Excellent! ... That's the way I like to see my suggestions carried out, m'boy.

Copyright 1943 Field Publications

157

No! We didn't lose a dog answering to the name of Rover. The ad was a ridiculous misprint....

That's the thirtieth call so far.

CROCKETT JOHNSON

Another person with a dog named Rover! Now I think I'm mad enough to tell that newspaper what I think of its stupid idiotic carelessness!

...and furthermore—hold on just a moment, please, until I get my breath....

Gosh!

Mom is balling out the newspaper, Mr. O'Malley. I guess she didn't get any results from that advertisement... even after you fixed it up.

Strange.

Copyright 1943 Field Publications

Mr. O'Malley.... I think you'd better wave your magic wand and make Gorgon's father appear and get it over with.

I'd do it at once, m'boy, but has it occurred to you that he may be, for all we know, a member of the armed forces? A K-9? And if I summoned him here he'd be AWOL?...

My father can't be a K-9.... He's a 4-F.

CROCKETT JOHNSON

He may have been reclassified.... No, I refuse to wave my wand until I know just where he is—

$\sqrt{FE} \div FI^2 \times FO =$

Look, m'boy.... Just the person who can figure that out for us—Atlas, the Mental Giant....

And he's got his slide rule working again...

FUMI

161

Mr O'Malley. When you waved your magic cigar in Hanson's barn and nothing happened—

WHEEEEEAAAAAAHH

Listen, m'boy! ...Fire sirens!

A fire. A costly conflagration. Probably caused by someone heedlessly dropping a lighted cigaret...Most fires are...One reason I stick to cigars.

Look! The engines!

They must be coming up to Hanson's farm—Say! Gosh! Mr. O'Malley! ...Your cigar! And that straw in the barn!

I don't see the point— Er—Cushlamochree!

But...Nonsense. Why, you just said nothing happened when I waved my wand—Look, m'boy. Splendid piece of fire-fighting apparatus...Nice color red...

CROCKETT JOHNSON Copyright 1943 Field Publications

Barnaby, are you accusing your old Fairy Godfather of being a pyromaniac?

Hook and ladder . . .

Certainly I'm not to blame if Farmer Hanson leaves a lot of inflammatory straw lying around his old barn.

The hose truck . . .

I see no connection between my attempt to find the father of this poor orphaned animal by waving my magic cigar, and—

The chief's car . . . And a fire dog!

FD

CROCKETT JOHNSON

IT'S MY FATHER!

Copyright 1943 Field Publications

165

170

171

Panel 1:

We didn't get NEAR that fire! An officious gendarme! He herded us off with a lot of gaping yokels!

Mr. O'Malley! . . . Mom doesn't want Rover! And he won't go back to the firehouse. . . .

7-8

Panel 2:

The ignorant fellow even refused to honor a press card clearly identifying me as a representative of the magazine "Smart Set."

He won't get out of the rocker on the porch. : . . He growls at Pop. . .

Panel 3:

ROCKETT
JOHNSON

Just shows the dwindling power of the press! In the days when I polished up Mencken's editorials for him—Eh? . . . What's that?

And he ate the meat in the icebox.

Panel 4:

He's been at the icebox? . . . Cushlamochree! Your folks can't tolerate that! Come, m'boy. Let's visit the scene of this intolerable crime!

175

For the last time, will you cease your intimidation of this child's parents and go back to the firehouse . . . ?

Arf.

He said "no."

I assumed his reply was in the negative, Gorgon. Well, m'boy, this impasse calls for drastic action!

With your wand and some magic words . . .

Copyright 1943 Field Publications

CROCKETT JOHNSON

So I suggest that you and your folks go away for the remainder of the summer!

Huh?

He'll experience the bitterness of a Pyrrhic victory and leave before you return in the fall . . .

Besides, your Fairy Godfather feels the need of a change of scene. . . . I'll get a handful of resort literature right away . . .

7-9

177

This sounds like the answer to our vacation problem, m'boy. A tour of the Orient! . . . "Visit Manila, Batavia, Singapore, Hongkong, Shanghai, Tokyo—"

Tokyo?

7-18

Does seem odd, doesn't it? . . . Unless the Marines have already—Say! What's this! "and you will treasure the memories of the winter of 1928"—Well! No wonder!

Hello, Jane.

That travel bureau! Handing out literature for winter trips in the summer! Lucky, isn't it, that your Fairy Godfather is such a discerning reader, or—

Gosh! ARE you, Jane?

CROCKETT JOHNSON

Mr. O'Malley! Jane is going on a vacation too! Maybe we could go where she's going.

Eh?

Mrs. Krump's Kiddie Kamp.

I wasn't able to find that Kiddie Kamp, Barnaby. It can't be much of a resort. . . . But I found a quaint old hostelry presided over by P. Callaghan, mine host. Here's one of his blotters. . .

For our vacation! A quiet retreat on Lake Echoechoecho—an old Indian name Callaghan made up. It means Echo Lake. . . I suggest You start packing immediately. . .

Gosh, Mr. O'Malley. It's a fine place. . . I'll tell Mom.

7-15

WELCOME

GENTS

INDOOR PICNIC GROUNDS

CALLAGHAN'S VALHALLA
P. CALLAGHAN, Prop.

ECHOECHOECHO
LAKE

OUTDOOR PICNIC GROUNDS
BASKET PARTIES WELCOME

**ROWBOATS &
POOL TABLES**

**LADIES INVITED
BAIT FOR SALE**

Entertainment Saturday Nites
Minimum Charge 40 Cents per Couple

ROOMS BY DAY OR WEEK

183

Mr. O'Malley, Mom doesn't seem to want me to go to that place you're going—

Callaghan's Valhalla?

She thinks Mrs. Krump's Kiddie Kamp is better...

Cushlamochree... No accounting for taste, is there?...

Well, I won't press the point... Your Fairy Godfather doesn't want to cause a rift in your happy little family... Inform your mother that I'll change all my plans. I'll go with you.

Gosh, Fine!

Copyright 1943 Field Publications

After all, this encampment for infants is on Echo Lake too... Not far from Callaghan's, and —But I must be off to select the proper outdoor equipment for our sojourn in the wilds...

CROCKETT JOHNSON

185

191

193

If O'Malley and I only had stayed at that hotel—

We're coming, Mr. O'Malley.

8-13

Now we'll have to rush back to Callaghan's and get you out of those wet clothes . . . Won't we?

Cushlamoglub!

Cushlamochree! . . . I can't be seen strolling through the stylish lobby of Callaghan's Valhalla in this condition . . .

Copyright 1943 Field Publications

Mr. Callaghan hasn't any guests besides you and me . . . Only that hermit in the bridal suite . . . But let us argue about it sitting down.

In that summer house.

CROCKETT JOHNSON

208

The police! ...Closing in on us! O'Malley, when we're arrested hadn't we better plead guilty and throw ourselves upon the mercy of the magistrate...

Plead guilty? Nonsense! We'll demand a jury trial! ... A dramatic court room struggle! ... My brilliant juridical mind ferreting out each hidden flaw in the prosecution's case and clamping on it like a steel trap! ... Surprise witnesses! Legal bombshells! ...Flashbulbs! ... Cries of "Objection!"...."Objection overruled!"

But Mr. O'Malley—

CROCKETT JOHNSON

My first shrewd move, Gus, will be a writ of habeas corpus—

But, O'Malley... That won't help me—a ghost—

Suppose I just go back to the Kiddie Kamp and tell Mrs. Krump we're sorry we took those chocolate bars.

Gus wouldn't come over today, Barnaby... He and that hermit are trying to make the hotel jukebox stop playing "My Wild Irish Rose"... After I worked so hard to get it going. Without nickels... Where's Mrs. Krump?

She went to answer the phone.

Leaving you and these other children unsupervised? Why, this is the sort of thing that causes juvenile delinquency! Lucky I happened to come by!

We're all right, Mr. O'Malley...

Shall I see how the children are?

I'm going right back to the playground... But they get on very well if they're left alone...

CROCKETT JOHNSON

My Fairy Godfather is going to supervise us.

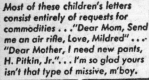

Most of these children's letters consist entirely of requests for commodities . . . "Dear Mom, Send me an air rifle, Love, Mildred" . . . "Dear Mother, I need new pants, H. Pitkin, Jr.". . . I'm so glad yours isn't that type of missive, m'boy.

8-26

Your mother will be pleased with its unselfish spirit . . . And doubly pleased by the magnanimity of the line I am about to append to it . . .

What's that?

A request . . . But for something you obviously don't desire for yourself . . . An altruistic and beneficent obtestation for—

For you? Okay, Mr. O'Malley.

CROCKETT JOHNSON

Are you leaving? You said you had a lot of big letters to write.

They're not important. . . . What if the "Times" DOES have to go to press with no letter column tomorrow . . .

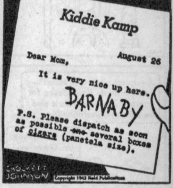